THIRTEEN DEPARTURES FROM THE MOON

Thirteen Departures
From the Moon

Poems

Deema K. Shehabi

Press 53
Winston-Salem

Press 53

PO Box 30314

Winston-Salem, NC 27130

First Edition

A TOM LOMBARDO POETRY SELECTION

Cover design by Kevin Morgan Watson & Sara Maher

Cover art, "Step Up," Copyright © 2011 by Harry Mijland

Printed on acid-free paper

ISBN 978-1-935708-23-0

for my parents,
Arwa Monir Al-Rayes (in memory)
and
Kazi H. Shehabi

CONTENTS

AKNOWLEDGMENTS   ix
INTRODUCTION BY TOM LOMBARDO   xi

I

Migrant Earth   3
The Glistening   4
Requiem for Arrival   6
Ghazal 1   12
In Mecca, When It Rains   14
Helwa's Stories   15
Light in the Orchard   19
Legends of the Bee   20
Portrait of Summer in Bossey, 15 Years Since   22
    Her Death

II

Lights Across the Dead Sea   29
Thirteen Departures From the Moon   31
Ghazal 2   35
Of Harvest and Flight   37
Blue   40
The Narrative   42
Qasida of Breath   45
Night Wind Through the Prison Window   46
At the Dome of the Rock   47

III

Flight Over Water   51
The Cemetery at Petit Saconnex   54
The Emptying   56
Green Fruit   58
Ghazal 3   60
Late Summer   61
Opal   62
Nahed   63
Ghazal 4   67
Khadijah   69
Curves in the Dark   72

Notes   75

Author biography   77

Cover Artist biography   79

ACKNOWLEDGMENTS

Atlanta Review : "In Mecca, When It Rains"
Banipal : "Legends of the Bee," "Ghazal 4"
Bat City Review : "Khadijah"
Callaloo : "Ghazal 3"
Canadian Journal of Environmental Education : "Blue," "The Emptying"
Crab Orchard Review : "Of Harvest and Flight," "Migrant Earth"
DMQ Review : "Opal"
Drunken Boat : "Portrait of Summer in Bossey," "Lights Across the Dead Sea"
Kenyon Review : "The Narrative"
Literary Imagination : "Thirteen Departures From the Moon"
Massachusetts Review : "Helwa's Stories"
Mississippi Review : "Requiem for Arrival," "At the Dome of the Rock"
Modern Poetry in Translation (England): "Ghazal 1" "Ghazal 2"
Perihelion : "Flight Over Water," "Light in the Orchard"

Additional thanks to the editors of the following journals and anthologies where some of the poems appeared (sometimes in different form): *Flyway, The Jordan Times Weekender, Meena Magazine, Siecle 21* (France), *Valparaiso Poetry Review, The Body Eclectic* (Henry Holt and Company, 2002), *White Ink: Poems on Mothers and Motherhood* (Demeter Press, 2007), *Birthed from Scorched Hearts: Women Respond to War* (Fulcrum Publishing, 2008), *Inclined to Speak: Contemporary Arab-American Poetry* (University of Arkansas Press, 2008), *The Poetry of Arab Women* (Interlink Books, 1998), *Letters to the World: Poems from the Wom-po Listserv* (Red Hen Press, 2007), *After Shocks: The Poetry of Recovery for Life-Shattering Events* (Sante Lucia Books, 2008), *Poets for Palestine* (Al Jisser Group, 2008), *The Space Between Our Footsteps: Poems and Paintings from the Middle*

East (Simon and Schuster, 1998), and *Poetry Daily*. The poem "At the Dome of the Rock" was made into a broadside by Paul Moxon of Fame or Shame Press and by Rhiannon Alpers for the Al-Mutanabbi Street Coalition as a benefit for Doctors Without Borders.

I wish to thank Elmaz Abinader, David Alpaugh, Beau Beausoleil, Hayan Charara, Cheryl Dumesnil, Persis Karim, Phil Metres, Donna Khorsheed, and Khaled Mattawa for their support. Much appreciation and thanks goes to Fady Joudah for his time and poetic agitations through the years. I am indebted to Marilyn Hacker for her wonderful collaborations, encouragements, and mentorship. Much gratitude also goes to the gentlemen at Press 53: Tom Lombardo (for his consummate editing and great suggestions) and Kevin Morgan Watson (for making it seem effortless). And to my husband, Omar Khorsheed, eternal gratitude, for his love and support.

Deema K. Shehabi
February 2011

Introduction

Deema K. Shehabi's poems root themselves in Gaza and travel through the entire breadth of the Palestinian diaspora. Herein are the stories of a displaced family—a metaphor for a displaced nation—passed down, passed down, passed down and told through the lush imagery of the Arab streets, the Gaza orchards, the fertile streams, all witnessed by the moon.

In her poems "Blue" and "Of Harvest and Flight," Ms. Shehabi writes, "Freedom is land," and since "the unbolting of our roots," Palestinians have not experienced freedom.

Most Palestinians who were separated from their homeland, now four generations later, still struggle beyond hope as an abstraction, many still in Gaza and the West Bank, some in Lebanon, a few in Kuwait, where Ms. Shehabi grew up, some in Egypt, many in Jordan, and others sprinkled across the remaining moon-circled globe, including California, where Ms. Shehabi lives today.

She writes in her poem "Curves in the Dark,"

> my child is asking:
> *how many moons did we leave behind?*

Thirteen Departures From the Moon will lock you into a strong sense of place, and you will feel the deep roots to a land that a people hold to as tightly as a 2,000-year-old olive tree digs for life. You will experience it through all five of your senses. You will come to understand Ms. Shehabi's definition of paradise in her poem "The Emptying":

> paradise is under the feet
> of your mothers.

I've never been to Gaza. After reading Ms. Shehabi's poems, I feel that I've visited there, that I've spent time with the people, and that I've walked her family's path from Gaza, through Kuwait, through Switzerland, to America. And always, the ever-present moon as guide.

In her notes page, Ms. Shehabi writes:

> In Arabic culture, it's the highest form of praise
> to compare one's beauty to the moon's.

Her collection is as bright, beautiful, and mysterious as the moon in all its phases. No matter where we live, nor how we live, on a clear night we can look up and be reassured.

Tom Lombardo
Poetry Series Editor
Press 53

I

MIGRANT EARTH

So tell me what you think of when the sky is ashen?

Mahmoud Darwish

I could tell you that listening is made for the ashen sky,
and instead of the muezzin's voice, which lingers
    like weeping at dawn,
I hear my own desire, as I lay my lips against my mother's cheek.

I kneel down beside her, recalling her pleas
the day she flung open the gates of her house
    for children fleeing from tanks.

My mother is from Gaza, but what do I know of the
    migrant earth,
as I enter a Gazan rooftop and perform ablutions in the ashen
    forehead of sky? As my soul journeys and wrinkles with
    homeland?

I could tell you that I parted with my mother at the country
    of skin. In the dream,
my lips were bruised, her body was whole again, and we danced
    naked in the street.

And no child understands absence past the softness
    of palms.

As though it is praise in my father's palms
as he washes my mother's body in the final ritual.

As though it is God's pulse that comes across
her face and disappears.

THE GLISTENING

There are mountains
that savor the sun at the end of day,
a sun drawn from the bludgeoned
belly of the East,
spilling bleeding streaks of exile
across the rocks.

There are mountains
that breathe the white light of autumn
into hospitals
where the comfort of swollen strangers
is a reunion with love.

In the dark, worn-out night,
mountains drip secret layers of perfumed mist
into the cheeks of young girls
and the moon is a solitary man
who waits in anguish
for the unveiling of violet courtyards
hidden just beneath the mountain tops.

Restless breathing mountains of the East,
enclosed in swells of desert light
tumble down, like moving hymns
into waiting lips,
of prayer-filled people.

Bountiful mountains of the West
hum softly into blue slumber
and rise past the valleys strewn
with the roots of wide-eyed children
creating a deep gnawing,
a love which makes you want to leave your skin behind.

And where is that mountain
the prophet wished for
to separate Mecca from its enemies,
that yellow mountain, face of black,
meteor of heaven?
I want to find that mountain
that will fold us inward slowly, that infinitely laboring
bald, beautiful mountain,
enemy of melancholy, ally of life
glistening darkly
in silence.

REQUIEM FOR ARRIVAL

Promise never to tell
that this is only a dream,

a morning dream, clipped by leaf's edge—
my mother leaning

against the balcony balustrade,

her hands migrating

      toward a jasmine flower,

her fingers enfolding it
              and bringing it slowly

to her freckled lips,

and she says: *Do not leave now that you are here—*
Stay, so the world may become itself again.

                ***

The world kept dwelling
in small rooms, dissonant sounds,

here below Mt. Diablo
where my child's eyes depose

the moon. In the valley,
he chases birds

through the lifts of hills,
and on certain nights,

I see another moonlit
                    refugee child

netting birds over
                    barbed-wire fences

***

Barbed-wire inscribes the blight
on the Holy City at dawn,

the rotten-plum light scalding
the mouths of fallen houses,

the seven-year-old boy surrendering
his belongings under a soldier's

tightly stitched breath,
prayers and burial lids

          arguing in the air—
and if the city dissolves the olive-tree

horizon as you look back,

promise never again to say:

the ancient skeleton of this house
once belonged to us

The air still trills
with the prescience of burial lids

even as I watch my child
standing here on a hill

at the edge of stars—

(the barrel-chested light
over the Holy City

never assumed such a form)
as we stood once

on the edge of a fresh mound,
where a woman once harvested jasmine

with the length of her fingers,
the words on her tombstone

still freshly inked
like dark rain:

We belong to God,
and to Him we return.

***

On the return, I entered
the temple of back rooms.

The black leather seats were ladders
descended from nowhere—

The interrogator confused

the pen in my wallet
for an exclusive remembrance

in disguise.

This is no silver arrival,
I told him.

The executioner's song

was full of praise,
but the child's song

snapped under the dawn's foot.

What toll is this, what bridge?
I passed men

whose mouths throbbed
with soil breath,
and beyond the glass

were long-rooted women
gazing at their unreachable orchards—

***

And the hills, too,
were long-rooted:

For every one gone to earth,
one hundred roots are planted.

***

The dawn faltered;

too much time had passed
in the stations

of sleep. Dawn's arrival:

you rose,
O how you rose
to greet me.

Always a house
with long green stairs,

fountain syllables
in courtyards.

Always a woman
more beautiful

than Lawrence
over Arabian sands—

her face
with its unmoored

longing for the sea

***

My child's hair is washed
in the sun's amaranth,

(orchard grasses churn winds
in the tomb of distance),

and his eyes chart
the same curved drowse

that my mother's once held.
So that the world

may become itself again,
will you stay awhile with me

and plant our grief in his hair?

GHAZAL 1

If I die, leave the balcony open.

Federico Garcia Lorca

Feet, young and old, tumble by then flee when the balcony opens,
but what about the house that seethes when the balcony opens?

Angels with daggers march through the funeral air of burned
children, and you're in the witness seat when the balcony opens.

I want to watch those voluptuous watermelons prune the ash,
says one angel, so for God's sake keep clear when the balcony opens.

We can't defend this pillow plump with insults, so we beat it down
before the jasmine convenes when the balcony opens.

Without the soil in Palestine, I'm bereft of planting,
soil of succulent green beans, wildly fleeting when the balcony opens.

The hour of magic cats dressed in lavender draws near;
look toward the horizon and halt your weave when the balcony opens.

Says Ondaatje: my love, punctual in green silk, brushes my face
with cinnamon and blurs it into my cheek when the balcony opens.

Let's double the batch of thyme bread before its scent pierces the earth,
before the dead hunger-heave when the balcony opens.

O brother, why not enter this room solidly with our right foot, ignoring
our torturers, as we fall to our knees when the balcony opens?

Transcendent poet, how will you tiptoe past a walled-in nation
that tramples the lapis lazuli when the balcony opens?

Pain dominates, says the father, but your smile bargains with that devil, and lightens loads for dreams when the balcony opens.

My sister ruffles the sky, cries the boy in the jeep, and my brother lies motionless beside me, but my body will burst into stream when the balcony opens.

O love, the length of your rib cage is my given fortune. Look how the twilight disrobes as I measure your needs when the balcony opens.

IN MECCA, WHEN IT RAINS

Hands, swollen and bruised, rot in the rain.

Faces sizzle in puddle mirrors.

Mecca of grit and full-throated drizzles:

here's a husband who unleashes his slippers

     at the gate—

Wife: tender as glued-on locusts

on black shimmering stone. *To feel the sacred bowstring, you must*

turn your body into an arrow, she says.

Oily finger prints

on the rain's half-light.

     Breathe out until breathing is skeletal.

Watch carefully as her palms

     dun the sky.

Maybe it's God who receives them

as they soar past the earth-ridden,

immovable pilgrims,

     dripping back down again

into this obsidian womb.

HELWA'S STORIES

1. The Fish

The cats rehearsed their jilted-courtesan cries
beneath the kitchen window. The glass broke,

and the Angel Gabriel cursed the sun,
which was carnivorous at noon. On those days,

I taught the child how to sweep the fish clean;
slice lengthwise through the belly,

use flour like water, pack mounds of salt
into the insides, remove its eyes

so it doesn't see the bramble of blood
in the dishpan—its iron scent is merely

a shiver beneath the nose.

2. The Soldier

There were holes the size of pigeons in our wall,
and we breathed in a constant whirl of feathers
and dust that had been snipped from our pillows.

I found the young soldier searching the house;
he was merely a boy, but he leaned forward with tethering eyes.
I locked him deep in the cellar and planted the key

in the cavity between my breasts where no hands dared
to tread. Ah the look of freedom as it flitted desperately
from his eyes—he promised never again to beat on our door

before dawn, never again before the tiny orange thread
appeared in the sky. He spent a whole day down there reciting
his dreams into ruins of rancid olive oil and dried-up yoghurt.

3. The Spirit of the Sheikh

His hair reeked of lemon cologne,
    and he had goat feet.

He held my tongue down with a muslin cloth
    because I shook a piece of the world

with my own hands. He trampled my shoulders,
    his bony knees against my ears

and demanded pounds of gold for forgiveness. To appease
    him, I took sugar from the pantry to the corner store

and traded it back for money. No-one believed
    me when I said that his eyes beamed more brightly than

a thousand blissful suns. They begged me to tell the truth
    because the child began to have nightmares.

I told them his heaviness was as unbearable as a tomb.
    And when he rode on my shoulders, I would forget

that I'm Helwa, the one whose honey-colored eyes
    could consume the sun's orange from the sky,

the one who could lace up free men with one spilled kiss.

4. The Earrings

Sometimes, the child would sit on the roof for hours
staring at the sun as it fell behind the muezzin's voice.
Often, the sky stared right back at her.
Often, when she returned, her forehead would be tattooed
with a few red poppies stolen by the wind
from a garden next to the sea. Sometimes, my craving
for shining things would return, and I would hide
her gold earrings for awhile—their glimmering
would fill the air, and I would close my eyes
and dream of the rich, glittering women
of Cairo as they walked through dusty streets
in their pressed white linen suits.

LIGHT IN THE ORCHARD

The black crows don't rise frequently from yellow fields
in sunset anymore though the sentiment does—you see
the earth as a trammeled garment beneath your feet and
the blue, teeth-marked cavity of water and sky circling around,
blue on copper, blue-green, green-auburn, and although
you wish to repent and say: *no country is worth fighting
for*—the rain light will suddenly riffle through the breeze
until finally you spot the swans bristling on the pond,
blood-colored clouds flaring in their black eyes,
and then away one last time to the orange grove,
where birds plight in your stall.

LEGENDS OF THE BEE

Body: be obedient in your yielding. I can't tell you what this
rapture means.

> *The gazelle girl picked at their hive with a stick. We rubbed her*
> *with garlic afterwards, barely hiding our joy, a blessing we*
> *said. The bee venom strengthened her body, injecting her*
> *with nature's blood, made from flowers, sun,*
> *air, and earth.*

What is death? A stained-glass jar where sun meets gold.

> *The fighter combed rough lands*
> *seeking the purest amber starch for his sick wife.*
> *He returned too late, but the orange liquid gave him*
> *clemency against remorse.*

Let's tell it like it is: I was never ready to lose you, over and
over again.

I can't dismantle the fear of the invisible.

> *The hawk-like tribesman would have died nine times, but he*
> *lived by eating a spoonful of honey at the crack*
> *of dawn. His chants still tease the air: O bee of blood,*
> *bee of light, bee of love, bee of death, bee of soul, O bee...*

Open the window to the orchard in the distance. I'm yielding
to the light.

> The cross-eyed boy placed his hand in a pond
> beneath a bee's thick needle, laughter turning to tears, as we rubbed
> garlic into wound. That was his first sting. Four bountiful stings
> in a lifetime we say, and then lavish healing.

PORTRAIT OF SUMMER IN BOSSEY,
15 YEARS SINCE HER DEATH

1.

When debris dissolves in the morning breeze,
I arrive to the house of half-breed poplars,
and my child says, *God lives at the far end of lightning*—

but here there are only rock shadows, arching clouds.
We bend and open to last night's visitor: my mother
on alabaster stairs, saying she has uncovered Gaza

in desiccant cracks of the earth. Her stories are currents
that glide out of her, gliding like my father
as he returns from towing the mountain behind him—

my bedroom window is wide open,
the earth is reeking of shallow sleep,
and he says, *There is no God but One.*

2.

What labors through shallow sleep? What aches in my mother?
She bows her dark ochre head to the lyrics
of Sabah Fakri: *It's been too long: I miss you as you are the light*

of my eyes, belling with water, as they followed her father
who walked to the podium with flowers strewn at his feet
to unveil Gaza's first statue of liberty? It later crumbled in the square—

first its plaintive shadow, then the hush of the crumble,
but she is not sure what salted the roots of his heart: the death of

her young sister or field upon field of exile—
he walked for weeks until he reached the border

of Lebanon, the sky rearranging the evidence of place behind him:
So I told her: let no guard stand in our way.
You've lighted my night, you most loved of visitors.

3.

Is this the calamity of roots? Are these the bleeding minutes,
the choked tendrils of love surrounding our life?
I tell my father that when she died, her oldest brother

carried a faint smile and said: *angels have brief respite on earth,*
but my father is too solemn for stories tonight.
Tomorrow they will chop down the blue-green spruce she planted—

it obstructs the view of the Geneva fountain
from the terrace, the fountain that purred and spun,
suddenly attacking passersby, my mother slipping,

her children and friends in slivers behind her.
For days, our bellies lunged towards laughter, but my father
is inaudible in the rain-lift of a night's storm.

4.

I carry her voice within me like all the living carry
the retreating voices of their dead, those white breaths
that we seldom hear unless we're afflicted: our arms swollen
with water, our breasts bleeding and blistering. Then other words sewn
into our mouths until the time comes when they
are unthreaded. The sobs of her oldest brother bending
and opening every doorway of the house. Her body washed
in the full light of afternoon.

5.

Were it not for the sudden blue-green gaze of sky,
I would have asked my father for a story,
and he would have told me he's known love.

6.

In the beginning, my brother and I plowed like Vikings
through the village of Bossey, finding the smoky dungeon
where the Duke tucked his enemies away from sunlight's disquieting

script on the horizon, from the scent of bruised apples
hidden beneath paper-soft trees, and from the rows
of crimson rose shrubs that atoned for all the violence

it took to make this place as beautiful as legend. We ignored
the sky as it crushed water on the blades of crosses, the blades bending
and opening. My brother and I chased sparrows that flew

towards the mountain. Later, we fell into the grass,
beneath billions of moon shards, our parents sitting on the terrace,
their sentences unthreading the dark.

7.

True story: my grandfather was the mayor of Gaza, a man who
walked where anyone would follow. He wrapped warnings around
his children: *If disgraced, I will sell my belongings and move to Switzerland.*
That my mother would be buried in a Swiss cemetery—wrapped
by a mountain that throws the sun back to clouds—he would
never know. I bathe her grave—sheets of cool water stored in
stone basins, all the while my ears pressed against the ambush of
words told long ago: *If she doesn't die young, I will cut my tongue out
and eat it.*

24

8.

Along rock shadow, my child and I stare at the purple flowers
that gallop towards the statue of mother cradling son,
the mother's face bending and opening to the grief
that hadn't yet materialized at that moment. *We're lost,*
I say, and my child is flying towards the sparrows,
as they glide across the mountain.

II

LIGHTS ACROSS THE DEAD SEA

Where were we
if not at the beginning?
The wind ambled
off the salt water,
the distance fractured our gaze
without a blink,
and the moon rushed
into the rouge of the hills.
Imagine, I said,
if those hills were still ours,
but you had already counted
the bone bites of a lost country,
opened each page
of those wounds to full glow.

The calm was too far off
to be remembered—
All around us: leftover stones,
look-alike orchards full
of lemons and guavas,
white bolts
of bandaged children—
morning still trembling on their lips,
their grassy lashes
glaring across makeshift coffins:
do we still carry those children in the blur

of the moon's afterglow?
At least they lived
and fought on their land, I said

recalling our last return—
was it the last?
when my mother soured the soldier's eyes
with her talk of blood
and the laws of its searing.
Then she loosened her forehead and said:
Look closely and you will still
see the etch of sweet sap
that comes from loving your land.

You crimped your breath
and held it in your mouth,
your eyes embering.
Listen, I told you, *this affection*
is not a failure,
while the lights across
the Dead Sea unsheathed,
guarding close their lowering sheen.

THIRTEEN DEPARTURES FROM THE MOON

1.

Whiter than memory—

Skeins of children in the pasture:

"Oh the full moon rose over us…"

tiniest petal, a smile in their eyes

2.

He hears the anthem
of moon-cadenced hills
banging
                    at the windowpanes:

"You're the name of what's in me of sleep,
So dream…"

3.

Upon your return
you will descend

through inland scapes
shorn of doorsteps

                    and welcome mats,

past towers of thyme
in yarrow-colored soil—

4.

Misshapen moon shawl
on her sloped shoulders

Hush, she says to quiet the chattering
angel of tides

5.

Night of angel collisions
at the foot of her bed

the smell of sugar and hair-ripped skin

The bride from Nablus writing her last letter—

The moon grips her eyes
as she looks up

from the veranda
where thistles grow

6.

Fields pecked ever so loosely by the sea:

"Ya amar, ana wi' yak

                    oh moon, you and I
companions since childhood, we loved our moon
you

          and I…"

7.

"The dead here hang in mid-air
until the moon
               breathes
                              out"

8.

Girls on swings
rising higher in the air

then knee-deep in the mud
one body splashed in the honeyed light

of used-to-be playgrounds:

treacherous moon
fire in the eye
of the sniper
who yawns after his bullets
dye the air

9.

Her voice belts your eyes that are bound
for every grief: "There are no boundaries
between you and the moon …"

10.

Outside Nablus
a smokeless moon

brushing the head
of a padlocked Mosque

11.

All these years
you and I (bereft of our bodies)

we saw how the moon
tethered our grave,
while the jinns extended their three thousand
hands upward

upward

12.

Pretend the jasmine between your fingers
is the key to a sovereign house
where only lovers of moon reside

13.

Find the belly
of the olive tree that rests
on the hillside between the well (its water inaudible now)
and the charcoal dust of that fallen Mosque—
there, if you look up through the silver-green leaves
you'll find a bride and a groom
biting back at the moon

GHAZAL 2

Your night is of lilac
Mahmoud Darwish

Who crosses the road at night in shawls of lilac?
Again, we'll lash out at the future with all our lilac.

The girl wails over her father's body on a beach that hives
with warships as though she's dressed in fireballs of lilac.

Laila, bitten by ferocious longing, absorbs the oiled blood
of Qays' jasmine, measures the deep-carved sprawl of his lilac.

O lover of tabla, your beat swelling with multitudes,
come rest your blue-veined hands on the scripted calls of lilac.

I will return one day, she says, to light the lamp of my snuffed-
out country, to translate the original protocol of lilac.

The Sufis say that everyone is to blame in a time of war
while they row their night boat towards waterfalls of lilac.

Shahid, how often did you "land on ashen tarmacs"
landing—then flying—your feet hauled by lilac?

Nothing is left for this parched earth where you are buried,
says the groom to his bride, except a rainfall of lilac.

If you don't let my son return to his mother, says the father
to the interrogator, your body will be mauled by lilac.

How we betrayed those summer clouds that crumpled our bed sheets;
our hasty unfolding, our constant footfalls toward lilac.

What have we lost, father, that can't be regained? What of our devotional yearning beneath the overgrown walls of lilac?

I don't want to break the dusk from where I stand, I say. The grass is too musky today, and the air enthralls with lilac.

OF HARVEST AND FLIGHT

Beneath a wet harvest of stars in a Gaza sky,
my mother tells me how orchards
once hid the breach of fallen oranges,
and how during a glowing night

of beseeching God in prayer,
when the night nets every breath
of every prayer,
my uncle, a child then, took flight

from the roof of the house.
The vigilant earth had softened
just before his body fell to the ground,
but there's no succumbing to flight's abandon.

Our bodies keep falling on mattresses,
piles of them are laid out on living room floors
to sleep wedding visitors:
the men in their gowns

taunt roosters until dusk,
while women hold the stillness
with liquid harvest in their eyes,
and night spirits and soldiers

continue to stampede through the house
between midnight and three in the morning.
On the night of my uncle's nuptial,
I watch my mother as she passes

a tray of cigarettes to rows of radiant guests
with a fuchsia flower in her hair.
Years before this, I found a photograph
of her sitting on my father's lap,

slender legs swept beneath her,
like willow filaments in river light.
His arm was firm around her waist;
his eyes bristled, as though the years of his youth

were borders holding him back
and waiting to be scattered.
Those were the years when my mother
drew curtains tightly over windows

to shut out the frost of the Potomac;
she sifted through pieces of news
with her chest hunched over a radio,
as though each piece when found

became a space
for holding our endless
debris. But in truth,
it was only 1967, during the war,

three years before I was born.
Tonight, I'm old enough
to listen to a story told my mother
in Gaza beneath the stars.

I turn toward her after she's finished
to ask how a daughter
can possibly grow beyond
her mother's flight.

There's no answer;
instead she leans over me
and points to the old wall:
the unbolting of our roots *there*,

beside this bitter lemon tree,
and here was the crumbling
of the house of jasmine
arching over doorways,

the house of roosters
and child-flight legends,
this house of girls
with eyes of simmering seeds.

BLUE

"The breeze that came down from over the hills was no longer."

Begin with your last gaze on the morning of your first departure,
your boyhood room in the hemorrhaging light, you combing
    your hair and staring
out the window at the sunken city of Jaffa, *Bride of the Sea.*

Scribble this little map on a torn napkin,
walk six blocks back from the sea, the house later found
behind a facade of ancient sepia,
and Donna says, "This must be Tata's house."

You say the sea will no longer cast its net on a city of vanished
    inhabitants.

Before we cross the Allenby Bridge, you tell me about your first
    leave taking:

> "When we first arrived at the dock,
> the gray-blue waves were large hills
>
> that opened to a thrumming sky, the sea swallowing
> the small boat, the big boat beckoning,
>
> but the sea would not take
> us across to Lebanon that day; its secret voice
>
> kept crying out to me:
> *Freedom is land.*

"Let's go to Nablus instead," your sister Hind said, "There's a
house there…"

Big house full of cold, stone walls that break a person in half.

"Which half are you after so much disassembly?"

Begin again with the story of your children's mother:

> "She rode that Tennessee Walking Horse regally
> at Little Daddy's Texas ranch, her back straight,
>
> her golden hair like an emissary of no known sun,
> her blue eyes unlike Mediterranean blue.
>
> I loved her since with all the darkness in my veins.
> Before I bought her a horse, I remembered how I
> sold cigarettes
>
> in the streets of Nablus. I bought Hind her first bra,
> and when I sold an entire carton, we ate lamb instead
> of vegetables."

On the morning of your first departure, loudspeakers blared news
of pregnant women with bayoneted bellies, and the dawn was
no longer dawn, and the breeze was no longer.

"Does that man with the restaurant on the water still serve fried
fish with lousy tahini?"

Omar sobs on the bus back to Jordan. The settlements
rush toward him. From over the hills, he feels a choking.
Donna says the blue of Palestinian pottery is unlike a blue
she's ever seen.

THE NARRATIVE

1.

Yehuda Amichai is pondering a cracked
ancient Jerusalem stone with his fingers—
no point in appeasing a stone, he whispers
as he rubs the obstinate,
light-lifting indentation
that punctuates its forehead—

Do stones have wombs, he wonders? Or can they be
sculpted into nests for birds?

2.

He serves bundles of stones
to the bent mourners:
this one is for the burial procession
around the olive groves;
this one for the lone smoky arm
left on the sidewalk;
this one for the half-deaf Arab who listens
to the whisper of stones
and smells in their skin
a heavenward thyme;
this one for each stolen fingerprint
taken at the airport.

3.

He tells the soldiers that his mother's house
once belonged to the dark—

there was not a single lit window
in those dark days, so much graying,

so little call from the birds,
and in coming to belong—

we made the desert bloom
we made the desert sing

until even these phantoms started
humming our national anthems

until these Jerusalem stones turned into crumbs;
each crumb our daily bread,

our daily bread a torrent of stones—

4.

We were once lost in a desert full of stones,
says his book of poems dangling from the soldier's pocket,
but there's a found hard happiness inside of us.

5.

He tells the soldiers to chew over his poems—
later, spit them in the wind until they land
over the stones—

6.

Sometimes, he feels like weeping
at the sight of some flown
blood-stained white shirt,
so he invites the stones
to join him in pondering
the clouds above—
is this air above Jerusalem full of prayers
or blackened corpses?

Sometimes, he remembers a place with no
stones—its beauty wrenches his imagination:
"Time-kissed hills above a blue bay,
where a hard happiness is found...."

QASIDA OF BREATH

The call to prayer at 5 a.m.
spreads my fingers over the scars of apple trees,
and the smell of sleepy earth in my love's hair
makes hummingbirds race
into the buds of fuschia.

Not so long ago,
the air grew soft
when the sun crawled from rock to cloud.

And I would pray to everything sacred
and I would bow and stare deeply at the earth
and walk through old cemeteries to find the dead softly gazing.

Sometimes, you breathe red poppies
over the hills in Palestine,
and I see girls with orchards
of almond trees in their eyes,
and old men strolling silently
among burned villages.

And I can't say how I love my people
and I can't tell my love how to leave our land without weeping
and I can't always love this land.

NIGHT WIND THROUGH THE PRISON WINDOW

after Annie Finch's "Name"

Bone white with black hair, undeliverable by photograph,
you dissolve as you lay over earth, your laminated
brows glowing in the sunken air
where you once watched stars luster

and disappear in the night breeze.
Stars luster, descend, lay over blanketed
coils. Will lustrous coils and small blankets beam
evening's cry to your distant children?

Evening's cry to the distant children,
what will become of me?
Forget me not, answered the children,
their bodies gusting against dark

playgrounds through the distance,
their playgrounds gusting

against dark bodies through the distance.

AT THE DOME OF THE ROCK

Jerusalem in the afternoon is the bitterness of two
hundred winter-bare olive trees fallen
in the distance. Jerusalem in the soft
afternoon is a woman sitting at the edge of the Mosque
with her dried-up knees tucked beneath her, listening to shipwrecks
of holy words. If you sit beside her under the stone arch
facing the Old City, beneath the lacquered air that hooks
into every crevice of skin, your blood will unleash
with her dreams, the Dome will undulate gold, and her exhausted
scars will gleam across her overly kissed forehead.
She will ask you to come closer, and when you do,
she will lift the sea of her arms from the furls
of her chest and say: *this is the dim sky I have
loved ever since I was a child.*

III

FLIGHT OVER WATER

Night:

The Syrian beach town
hunches over a gauzy moon

     and curves against the sky

A blanket of cave walls
opens over our bodies

Water in the blood
    then waves—

Deep Night:

Mosquitoes on catamarans
colonize our arms

    Wetness procrastinates
our stifling at death

Impermanence:

Someone's boat condenses
    our breath

    in the basalt shells

We blunt our eyes out with sand
        and block out deep ponds
of stillness

Morning's Desire:

A cold, pillared corpse kiss

        I'm still a vagrant in your arms,
says the wave

        Shore's freeze
in the back of your mouth

Prophesy:

I can't   *(ebb)*

hide

my disgust   *(flow)*

at death

even for   *(ebb)*

a day
                (flow)

Noon:

A verse throws anchor into our tongues:

O God, most compassionate, most...

52

Late Afternoon:

The sunless artillery
of your voice:

no more,
here, with you.

Sunset:

Long ago, in Ra'as Al-Baseet

two children entered the sea,

their cheeks were buoyant apples

their lips bowed down
            to the dusky water

Impulse:

Look: there's amber

through the trees

Twilight:

Your eyes petition a gnarl
in the star:

Wait forty days, *oh wobbly grief...*

THE CEMETERY AT PETIT SACONNEX

No earthbound morning is this
when we walk together
past the huge exalted folds of tombstones
through an open wild mist that severs our throats
and a deep green so warm like love
past the Christian and Jewish quarters
to a piece of earth where we, too, bury our dead.

We talk of tombstone colors
in hushed intimate tones
you do not like gray
it does not breathe.

We climb a little and approach the spot
where the soil spreads like water
over her body.
We lift our palms to pray,
but all I can think of is you in 1962
a proud man with a wound of some sort
bending to a moon layered with migrant hymns on the Potomac
dreaming of the claylike swell of the Nile
stripped by the warmth in the play of her eyes.

I see you resting beneath eucalyptus trees
your head on her lap
your sleep filled with breezy afternoon dreams.

And through this trembling I swear

I see beautiful floods
just beneath the crescent of my brother's eyes
waiting, unnamed,
the translucent love bond between mother and son.

My mother's voice rises above the sound of waterfalls,
past a thousand orchards
of love;
she sheds the tread of pain imprisoned in her body
and drops beside you
depositing petals
that glow melancholy in your ear.

THE EMPTYING

Whenever we buried the sun's palm
in our mothers' eyes
my grandmother would quote the Prophet,
the white butterfly in her voice
dragging over red-haired grass:
paradise is under the feet
of your mothers.

She never wanted to bury our mothers
each in a country
under a sun that hung
the eye of envy,
its heavy arrow darting
toward them through the years.

We only wanted to be there at the beginning
when she rode her donkey to school,
Jerusalem's golden Dome crowned
in the black mink of her hair,
and when she lamented a love poem by Byron,
and later when she lined up her daughters
in front of a mirror: *You are not as beautiful*
as others, but your eyes are like the long rays of the sun.

Those summers she reclaimed the sun
with eyes like giant cups of dew
swaying beneath the blue-green spruce,
as we flooded at her feet
listening to her stories of lustrous jinns,
who hide the earrings of little girls.

She said the angel of death
would arrive disguised as the eye of fog
to escort those post-amber, sulky souls,
and that he would carry a lantern so sooted
that even the sun could not cleanse.

How does the eye empty the spirit
when the time comes?
we asked, as we slipped
on the delicate skulls of her warnings,
and she smoothed out our knotted eyebrows
with her open fingers in the sun.

GREEN FRUIT

after Pablo Neruda's "Walking Around"

It so happens I am happy to be a daughter
and it happens that I dance into dinner parties
and Arabic concerts,
dressed-up, polished like a pearl
in the tender hands of a diver
sliding on my path in a garden of olive trees and jasmine.

The scent of my mother sends me to a green orchard.
My only wish is to grow like seeds or trees.
My only wish is to see no more death, no poverty,
no more maimed, no drunks, no drugs.

It so happens I am delighted
by my father's victories and his pride
and his brown eyes and his bald head.
It so happens he is happy to be my father.

And I'd feel lucky
if I attended my parents' 50th wedding anniversary
or conceived a child with dark curly hair.
It would be wonderful to free my country with honest talk
planting orange trees until I died of happiness.

I want to go on following the moon—
bright, silvery, secure with the light
casting jasmine into the bloody streets of Jerusalem,
blossoming every day.

I don't want to fall in a grave,
restless beneath the weight,
a martyr for nothing,
dried-up, battling against the lies.

That's why my mother when she greets me
with her outstretched arms gives me the moon,
and she runs through the arching streets of Gaza,
and stops to stare at the white minarets of the mosques,
planting seeds of green fruit.

And my father leads me to the Golden Dome of the Rock
into debates about survival
into gatherings where friends speak of the good past
into houses that remind me of home
into a sunny shelter where doorsteps
are fragrant and windows rise to poplars.

There are starving children, and homeless people
hovering in the polluted air that I hate.
There are malignant cysts
that should disappear from bodies and skin.
There are soldiers all over, and machine guns, and tear gas.

I climb slowly with my moon, my roots, my dome,
remembering my parents,
I hike up through the sloping hills and green orchards
and gardens of olive trees smelling of jasmine
in which little white petals are growing.

GHAZAL 3

Mt. Diablo's snowy peak dips into the skin; *oh* that lull in the distance.
In the valley, the soccer mom snaps at her son as he falls in the distance.

I'm still as fierce and unconquerable as the Tigris, she says,
and I'll flow backwards in time to return to Mosul in the distance.

O tribes of this land, we, too, saw morning's flare in the palm lines
of children; their eyes interrogated our useless vigil in the distance.

Songs criss-crossed in the wind through willowed thickets
where the homeless child once slept on a thistle in the distance.

Thieving bird, what's the name for this ecology: your feathers
gusting on a tenebrous leaf skull in the distance?

What's in a name? Neither hands, nor feet, says the master poet,
but we fought to name our lands when we were youthful in the distance.

How many of you here actually believe in God, asked the child,
and what of the spider and his epic webs that still tremble in the distance?

Pray for me, dear pilgrim, as I have forgotten God in the midst of
these bountiful curves, and I feel so unworthy of this sacred toil in the distance.

Whom do you blame for disasters outside or within your borders: the sick,
the dying, or the conqueror within? Threats that triple in the distance!

LATE SUMMER

My bony child drowns the grass
with a loose-headed hose
then hangs one-limbed from the crepe
myrtle branch: "I   smell   benzene   in   the   leaf   curls."
My second child whistles; his breath
spews tiny windows into thick-skinned apples,
and my husband says: *a complete   garden   is   death*
to the imagination.

Across the street, the lone neighbor chokes
on the incandescent horizon. Instead of light,
he sees the burning. He jingles
his saw and grinds five rose bushes
down to the ground. Slowly, he shreds
the dark blue, "*Good evening!*"
Blood petals   blood-litter
his mouth—

OPAL

Here is the light loosening through the leaves.
It makes its way past a morning that resembles,

in its sever of bird song and scent of old-wood smoke,
every place and no place we know. You point

at those roots resting beneath the enormous Aleppo pine
and say they are the ancient calligraphy aging

on mosque corridors. You say roots are leaping market places
sprawling in a thousand directions, and those wrinkles emanating

endlessly from my forehead. And what of roots we find in small
hands, beneath big feet, succumbing to an earth that leans inward

and opens to a sky withdrawn from stars? Here, we yellow
when we think of our dead, and we grow large with rootlessness,

although our blossoming is born. What kind of hunger is it,
our bathing in the mist of all this light?

NAHED

(i)

The muezzin gripped
the minaret's head,
and dipped it into the sea

water in the submerged
prayer's voice
rushed ahead

a voice like water
reached the cemetery
deep within the city

(ii)

They didn't believe
he crushed a girl's
ribs with just one hug

They didn't believe he crushed
her ribs in an orchard
full of pines

(iii)

She forbade the children
to shout his name
across the house walls—

Instead, whisper it to the grapevine,
where salt in its veins will mix
with tears cried over him

and strangle the gardener's nose

(iv)

He pricked her with a poem
for his dead mother
then composed a wedding song

for the newlyweds
and stitched it across the sky
between the moon balcony

and pink jasmine
between Jerusalem and Gaza
between the olive and lemon

(v)

I want to break this house with sobs,
he said, each sob for a lost sister,
each sister a blossom from the vine of lady bank's rose

(vi)

Heat from the sea's sun
condensed the sweat
on his forehead

which fell into a poppy
that grew out of a rock
as seen by a tourist from Norway

(vii)

Her head on his chest
next to a bubbling fountain on a Sunday
in a garden in Damascus

his voice muffled
the faint cries
of the tortured in the wind

(viii)

Faith can't be measured
by how far an eye
can see,

he said to her once
as she wiped mascara
from her eyelids

(ix)

She said to his son
as he walked along the pier,

"I was selling sardines
at the fish market
with my 10 children,

and he gave me
a box full of lemons,
oranges, and grapefruit

from a heavenly orchard."

(x)

"How could you allow
a womb full of adjectives
to break off from my body?"

she whispered
as they swung low

on a hammock in autumn

GHAZAL 4

How sullen we've become in the belly of the empire;
nobody wrestles time for afternoon tea and honey in
    the empire.

What trumpets behind the fence? Orange-bellied birds in
    magnolia
blossoms, skittery squirrels, it's spring in the sunny empire.

On MLK day, the children pack tuna sandwiches and apples
for the tent-city homeless who are going hungry in the empire.

Foggy morning in Oakland, the scent of deep-fish frying, and
    the newspaper says:
Koreans fly home to avoid expensive denistry in the empire.

Body scanners, fingerprints, cameras on street corners—
airports have become dangerous places for Sunnis in the empire.

Friends pat me on the back, *enjoy what you have*;
distances between people have nothing to do with money in
    the empire.

Once, we rushed to the North End for succulent Italian.
Now, even the Irish neighborhoods serve up minestrone in
    the empire.

Who'd clip a foreign tongue and chop off a last name?
    Acculturation means men
with erased accents listen with vigor to Limbaugh's litany in
    the empire.

She hears May Nasr's song to Gaza, reads Hacker's translations
of Venus Khoury Ghata and deposes a desire to give it up
totally in the empire.

KHADIJAH

How tied-up he must be,
his every word orphaned
by the dialect of night statues.

So much silence
from such a human man,
as though his entire existence
relied on listening.

And look how
from out of the sky
the wind's loose rake arrives,
gathering him gently
through the insomnia of night.

He was just a little boy
when I saw him last,
and even then, his eyes
were embankments of light.

This was before I became a widow,
before my children whirled
and spun out of the large
lit-up meadow of my youth.

We were thriving then,
the earth still giving,
the sky dissolving gently
as it entered dark-leaf doorways.

Days now, I wait in bed dreamless
until the desert's sulphured light
traces the lines
on the inside of my hand,
the whole of me stretched out

and listening.
I hear something:
so unlike weeping,
so unlike the hollow
shout of statues
that deafen Mecca

and crack the smooth
silhouette of the dark.
I hear, but I cannot tell you
what it is.

I feel cindery warmth;
it is merciful
and pulls me towards its center.
When I stand where twilight
meets rain,

watching the birds throw bits
of messages to clouds,
the sky opens
with no warning.

And I think of the large
stroke of loss
that inhabits my life,
but have I become a woman

so fractured
and preoccupied only
with my own mending?
Tell me: how is it possible
to see past a death
that shines

in front of our eyes?
But the light
in Mohammed's eyes
is a large vessel
that does not carry me
to the drown
of graveyards.

It leaps through me,
eavesdrops on my oneness
and leaps higher,
holding itself there.

CURVES IN THE DARK

There will be no creeks left
in the hills below Diablo mountain.
No blowsy almond orchards

or rust-purple grass before green;
No one will come to us and ask:
Do you recall the struggle

of moon-veined blossoms
and the carnage of deer
in this thinned-out valley?

No gray-haired woman will be left
to tell a flood of warm-eyed children:
Weave those acorns back through the leaves

so they can be found by animals starved by winter.
And you thought the Iraqi moon
high above palms

would fall over our fragments,
and this live oak you placed in California earth
would give us refuge

against shadowed rustling,
but this moon is neighbor to everyone,
barefooted blade of silver

searching for a flawed heart to swell.
I touch the chill in my forehead
and wonder what it would be like to lose all my hair:

Jasmine with your knife of scent:
I hope my child never has to kneel
over my grave and weep

beneath a sleepless flesh of sky.
And you thought these weight-filled branches
would braid themselves

against the roof and root this house to earth,
but how often have we tugged
at curves in the dark

to remake our scars and slay our death?
Here the truck sounds are unhealed,
like all our comings and goings,

but what of making a home, you ask?
while across the street the bulldozer
flattens the torso of the last almond tree.

Tomorrow they will flatten Fallujah,
the newswoman says swiftly—no sign
of carnage in her eyes,

and through the stomach
of the house, my child is asking:
how many moons did we leave behind?

NOTES

In "Requiem for Arrival" the italicized line "Do not leave know that you are here. Stay—so the world may become itself again" is from Faiz Ahmed Faiz's poem, "Before You Came," as translated by Agha Shahid Ali (*The Rebel's Silhouette: Selected Poems*, University of Massachusetts Press, June 1995). In section 3, the italicized line "We belong to God, and to Him we Return" is from the Quran. In the sixth stanza, the italicized line "For every one gone to earth, one hundred roots are planted," is a traditional Palestinian peasant saying. In section 5, the italicized line, "The executioner's song was full of praise" was adapted from a line in Adam Zagajewski's poem "Try to Praise the Mutilated World", as translated by Clare Cavanaugh (*Without End: New and Selected Poems*, Farrar, Straus, and Giroux, March 2003).

In "Thirteen Departures from the Moon" in section 1, "Oh the full moon rose over us," is a religious song, which is sung by children in Muslim countries during the Eid festival. In section 2, the line in quotations "You're the name of what's in me of sleep, so dream..." is from Mahmoud Darwish's "Sonnet IV", as translated by Fady Joudah (*The Butterfly's Burden*, Copper Canyon Press, August 2006). Also, in section 6, the lines in quotations "Ya amar ana wi-yak" are sung by the Lebanese singer, Fairuz, and lyrics are by the Rahbani brothers. In Arabic culture, it's the highest form of praise to compare one's beauty to the moon's.

"Khadijah" is name of the Prophet Mohammed's first wife, the first woman to convert to Islam, and a loved and revered figure in Islamic history. The line "...fractured and preoccupied with one's own mending" is a line from Frank Gaspar's poem: "It's the Nature of the Wing." (*Night of a Thousand Blossoms*, Alice James Books, April 2004).

The title "Curves in the Dark" is from a line in W.G. Sebald's long poem "After Nature." (*After Nature*, Modern Library, July 2003)

The poem, "Ghazal 1" is for Najwa AbuKhadra.

The poem, "Ghazal 2" is for Marilyn Hacker.

The poem, "Blue" is for Fuad Khorsheed and Donna Khorsheed.

The poem, "Qasida of Breath" is for Jumana Husseini.

The poem, "Flight Over Water" is for Hashem Shehabi.

The poem, "Ghazal 3" is for Wafaa' Zein Al-Abidin.

The poem, "The Emptying" is for Suheila Shehabi.

The poem, "Nahed" is for Nahed Monir Al-Rayes.

The poems, "Lights Across the Dead Sea," "Curves in the Dark," and "Opal" are for Omar Khorsheed.

DEEMA K. SHEHABI is a poet, writer, and editor. She grew up in the Arab world and attended college in the US, where she received an MS in journalism. Her poems have appeared widely in journals and anthologies such as *The Kenyon Review, Literary Imagination, New Letters, Callaloo, Massachusetts Review, Perihelion, Drunken Boat, Bat City Review, Inclined to Speak: An Anthology of Contemporary Arab American Poetry,* and *the Poetry of Arab Women.* Her poems have been nominated for a Pushcart prize three times, and she served as Vice-President for the Radius of Arab-American Writers (RAWI) between 2007 and 2010. She currently resides in Northern California with her husband and two sons.

For further information about Deema, please visit: www.redroom.com/member-my-writing/dkshehabi

Cover artist **HARRY MIJLAND** is an amateur photographer who finds inspiration in the landscapes he is familiar with: the flat Dutch countryside he cycles through to work, and the seascapes and beaches of Northern Spain where his wife was born. "Photography," he states, "is too much fun to leave to the professionals."

To see more of Harry's work, visit:
www.flickr.com/photos/dearharry/